ANOTHER REVOLUTION

NATHANIEL ROBERT WINTERS

BUFFALO PRINTING COMPANY
Napa Valley California

Acknowledgements

I owe my writing chops to many.

First and foremost is my major muse, my lovely wife, Colleen.

The Thursday morning Solstice Writers have shared their collective knowledge about rhyme and verse with me for six years. It has been my pleasure to exchange so many laughs and tears with them.

I have also been a participant in many of Ana Manwaring's writing classes. Thank you Ana and all the students for giving your thoughts on my poetry and prose.

Cathy Carsell, my editor and proof reader has been an invaluable helper.

As a dual member of Napa and Redwood Writers, I've felt the backing of these two organizations of the California Writers Club that traces its roots back to Jack London and Joaquin Miller. My short stories and poems have found a home in their newsletters and anthologies.

I've had the support of friends, family, and fans of my many writings.

Thank you all.

Introduction

I was asked the other day (August 2017) at the Napa Valley Writers Conference if I was a poet. I was never asked that question directly before.

I've been writing and sharing poetry for many years. Yet I thought of myself as a story writer first. So, am I a poet?

A poet can tell a story.
Poetry invades your soul.
It brings music and magic to your words.
Poetry attempts to answer questions with no answers.
Poetry can bring the outdoors--inside and the indoors--outside.
A poet can make you laugh and cry.
A poet has romance in his heart and humor up his sleeve.
Poetry challenges the status-quo or can defend the establishment.
Poetry is art.

Three years ago I wrote and published a poetry book entitled, **The Poet I Did Not Know.**
I know myself much better now.

So am I a poet?
Yes, I believe I am.

I invite you to read **Another Revolution** *and decide for yourself.*

Table of Contents

Another Revolution

Earth completes another circle around the sun,
another year passes.
It's New Year's Eve 2017
Fireworks shot high into the sky, explode in
celebration.
Bombs and missiles fall from air, explode with
destruction.
They-we won't give peace a chance;
that was just a dream some of us had.
What are they-we fighting for, this time?
The usual suspects:
religion, territory, oil, water?
Do we need a reason?
Donald Trump spews hate like Hitler
Americans flock to him, like he's the messiah.

Even inner-city kids with so much in common,
join gangs and choose up sides to hate, red or blue.

I approach another birthday, still with hope.
Winter solstice has past, days get longer.
Rain falls on dry California.
I stay the eternal optimist
Peace on earth

Poems about my home:

I live in a special space.
The unique wine growing region, Napa Valley,
a part of the San Francisco Bay Area
and
The Redwood Empire of
Northern California,

in that special biosphere of planet earth.

Home

2015

Our house in Saint Helena
fits me like an old shoe.
new paint a spit shine
and she looks good
built in the 50's ranch style
much like the one I grew up
in Green Acres on Cloverfield Rd.
I almost awake expecting to see
Mom, Dad, Liz, Ellen, Fred and Doug

Now I wake to see my wonderful wife
Colleen and commuter college son, Sam
I walk in green acres
with hills covered in fields of clover
golden mustard and grape vines
my daily walk to the Napa River
could be Mill Creek

I look at Mount St. Helena
towering to the north
and the hills filled with redwoods
a very different green acres
I love to call my home

Epicenters

11- 12 - 14

Despite rumors of my demise
it would appear I will reach 65
I can't go wrong when I write
with prose and poetry I don't feel up tight

I fell in love with San Francisco Bay
faults and all, I came to stay
no way to see, would come a day
our epicenters did match—that's the catch

Drought, Earthquakes, Forest Fires and other Unnatural Disasters

Climate change will probably be the biggest problem of the next generation.

Why did I quantify it with a probably?
"Because it just goes to show you, it's always something," as Roseanna Danna used to say.
Yet with all the mountains of scientific evidence that we have been increasing carbon in the atmosphere, causing a greenhouse effect, there are deniers.

Why?

When people deny science it's usually tied to money. Remember all the tobacco company deniers of cancer evidence.

Now its big oil and other big carbon burners turn.

Smoky Sunshine

August 3, 2015

Walking along grape vines
the valley is an island of sunshine
smiling down from a clear brilliant blue sky

fog splashes over Western Mayacamas Mountains
like a Pacific ocean wave
eastern hills cling desperately to mist's moisture

But looking north, Mt Saint Helena
billows smoke, spewing evil black clouds
like a volcanic cinder cone

Fire consumes drought dry flora
driving desperate droves
to flee fields and homes

An army of the brave
fight flames from air and ground
making little headway against the torrent

Taste smoky tears
as they fall from my face
I watch helpless

November 2015 Endangered

A tune played on my phone, you know it
from Paul Simon, songwriter and poet
a little ditty all about a zoo
a favorite place for me to view

I know his song was all metaphor
not this, the zoo I do adore
often, I took son Sam and friend
to the zoo in the hills above Oakland

Lined with trees, Eucalyptus from down under
enclosures contained worldwide species of wonder
lions, hippos, monkeys
cheetah with powerful thighs
but my favorite were the elephants
with those intelligent eyes

Illegal poaching, government officials' greed
fill trophy hunters and ivory dealer's needs
his horn false aphrodisiac,
rhino's blood runs red
until whole species are left for dead

"Yes it's all happening at the zoo,
I do believe it's true,"
it may be the last place to go
to see the animals we used to know

A New Nobility

Harvest descends on the rich fields of wine grapes
like hordes of history's miners
finding gold nuggets of Chardonnay

Juices of blood red Cabernet are sluiced
capturing each valuable drop

Every earthly orbit of the sun
two million tourists swarm like honeybees
devouring narcotic nectar of the vines

New castles crown Napa hills
home to a new royalty
Mondavi and Montana

Happy drunk euros, yen and yuan
join green dollars
fill tasting room cash registers

Empty pockets stagger home

With lips kissed by honey

expensive the taste of beauty

Nouveau riche farmers look nervously
to the skies
in hope of winter's rains

Listening to the Wind

There is a consistent inconsistency to the rhythm of
the wind,
it whistles by in dots and dashes like crazy Morse-code
as it blows the icy cold ocean fog into the Bay and San
Francisco.
Cash registers clink as frozen summer tourists buy
sweatshirts at the wharf.

Grit glides by ears as swirling sand sprays buildings
like a snare drum.
Clothing ruffles and girls laughingly scream as they
pat their skirts back down.
Ferryboats ratta-tat into wind driven waves that
splash in the Bay.
Blinding fog causes horns to blow below the Golden
Gate Bridge

The wind picks up a Latin beat as it blasts beyond the
Mission District.
It carries the blues from North Beach on the click of
chop-sticks in Chinatown,
rock and rolls down Market Street and kicks up a
cheer at AT&T Park.
The gale flows over Nob Hill then races the clanging
cable-cars down.

Listen how the wind whips by the next time you're in San Francisco.
Dance to the consistent-inconsistency of its rhythm.
It might help keep you warm.

Finding Sunshine

Into my life she came
a full blown hurricane
winds at full blast
tried to hold on fast

Two days before becoming nine
like it or not she was mine
my new mother
could there be another

Into her house came we three
father, sister, me.
How does one learn
to love a hawk when you're a dove?

Dad loved her, he did
even during shouting, screaming
tried to disappear dreaming
from the abuse I hid

Stayed away dawn to twilight
home felt very dark at night
it's hard to become
when you've lost where you're from

Somehow made my way
past the time of play
three thousand miles away
where I came to stay

There was the adult me
the person I came to be
under a redwood tree
finally totally free

A child so lost
came to be found
a ball that bounces
can roll around

Eden Exists

North of San Francisco, beyond the Golden Gate
Eden exists in a land called Napa

In the valley, wine grapes grow
from North edge of the Bay
to fertile feet of Mt. Saint Helena
as far as a golden eagle eye
can see when she soars

An agricultural preserve, unique
saved from development by those with vision
conservative and liberal
farmer and environmentalist
agreeing not to always agree

The forested hills tower east and west
filled with redwoods and native hardwoods
deer, raccoon, fox and cougar abound
in natures playground

North of San Francisco, beyond the Golden Gate
Eden exists in a land called Napa

Meanwhile my mind moves back to my first home, New York.

A New Dawn

All through the winter of 1968 girls were required to
wear skirts or dresses to school
before the social revolution came to Valley Stream
South High School.
Dawn arrived early for Laura that fateful day with
frost covering the ground
 on a bitter cold morning.
She looked at the skirt her mom had laid out for her to
wear and she shook her head.
She put on pants instead.
Just the thought of walking that frozen mile sent
shivers up her spine.
 Laura knew it was time to learn a new game.
All eyes turned to her as she walked down the hall.

Mr. Burgin, the principal noticed her attire immediately and took her to the office.

"Young lady," he said, "you know that girls are not allowed to wear pants at school."

Laura raised her head in defiance and said, "I think it's quite time for a change."

"Rules are rules and girls should dress as girls." The principal insisted, "Therefore you are suspended from school today. When you come back to school tomorrow, you must dress appropriately. Understood?"

"No sir, I don't think you understand." She said defiantly.

The very next day all the girls came to school wearing pants.

Laura proudly said, "Our clothing should not be determined by an X-chromosome."

"Yes! We are with you!" The students shouted.

Mr. Burgin just shook his head. "This place has become a Zoo."

The social revolution had reached suburbia.

Oh My, I Want Pizza Pie
from New York please
so delightfully delicious
all you need on top is cheese

by the slice or a whole pie
I usually eat a lot
careful don't burn your mouth
out of the oven it's very hot

Born in Italy
City of Naples
Immigrated to New York
to become one of our staples

Chicago style is very good
but it's heavy and so square
that you can't make a show
of tossing and stretching the dough

In California we go crazy for toppings
some eat it with knife and fork
or get gourmet and add sprouts
give that to me, I'll throw it out

I want the original
New York style please
Thin crust, red sauce and lots of cheese

Meeting Mother Nature

Catching up on an old story
Mother Nature called,
"Come share my glory."

In spring and summer of '73
didn't yet write poetry
finished Junior College, was totally free
so took off for the mountains;
Ripple-dog and me

In his pack he carried food
Mine had all essentials, very crude
Set off in no particular order
from Mexico to the Canadian border

Ventana, Desolation, Olympics, Cascade Crest
All the major mountains of the far West
My dog led, I followed his tail
Over granite peeks along many trails

How far today boy? 15, 20 miles
Whatever; he would say with a silent smile
Dry, thirsty, hungry, or wet;
went hiking for weeks
over log river bridges,

fording fast running creeks

As August's days grew late
time to leave for important date
to meet my fate
at the school Sonoma State
to become the future me,
and find my destiny

Art of Loving

Birds do it, bees do it,
even educated flees do it
or may bee not.
This bee not a lesson about human sexuality
but something more important, survival.
Flowers have male parts called anthers containing
pollen
pistils are female parts
The roses are singing, "mother was a pistil
I'm a son of a gun."
Flowers need bees to pollenate
but pesticides and pollution
have decimated bumblebee and bird populations
like some Alfred Hitchcock movie.
Without the birds and bees no flowers appear
food becomes scarce
animals and man become endangered
love can't bloom.
Remember Shakespeare's ominous warning
To bee or not to bee?
That is the question.

The Eaglet

The eaglet perches
on edge of the nest
has tested his wings

They are strong

knows right from wrong

bigger then both parents

Take that final leap

catch the thermal wind

Soar

The Quench

Quenching rain falls

Perilous plants drink

Animals stop give thanks

Wet Winter Blues

On my morning walk to the river
in soggy socks water soaked boots,
I watch evil gray storm clouds
spill over the Mayacamus Mountains
drenching us with another deluge.

Saturated dirt drifts downhill
falling as avalanches
covering local roads
like mountains of snow covered Sierra

Swollen Napa River overflows its banks
flooding homes and Silverado Trail highway.
Did Mother Nature have to make up for
five years of drought in just one winter?

In this darkness of cold gloomy winter,
a sadness grabs me.
I remember earth's northern half,
starts its tilt towards the warmth of summer
with a promise smiles
and sunny days ahead

The Four Seasons

(Not Frankie Valli's Group)

Summer

Summer's so very sexy
long tanned legs stretch naked
below thin fabric - tiny cups - scarlet red bikini
sun touches flesh perspiration appears
skin glows uninhibited sensual
dark sunglasses hide sky-blue eyes
golden-blond locks shimmer
like sunflower petal's floral display
boys buzz by like honeybees

She leads latest toy to shade
under boardwalk she steals a kiss
smiles amused then devours him
above hot dogs sizzle on the grill
french fries dive into steaming oil
she encourages exploration of hills and valleys
like he's a sports car driving the coastal highway
Sun slowly sinks until swimming
aglow in waves of cold water
Summer sashays away hips swaying
too cool to turn
throws hand up waves goodbye

Autumn

Autumn starts golden like
the coat of Alaskan grizzly bear, guzzling salmon
California chardonnay grapes
New York granny smith apples
prairie's endless acres of corn and wheat waving
mountain aspens join the parade shake from green to
gold
soon lower elevation deciduous trees turn blond
like beached starlet want-a-be the next Marilyn,
sauntering down Hollywood Blvd.

Harvests speaks Spanish,
yellow bandanas shading golden glow under sweaty
sun
crops safely stored,
tree and vine leaves become a kaleidoscope of color
New England countryside an impressionist's dream
days get shorter leaves dim-darker
finally falling to blow in the wind
like ship's storm flags
warning of weather to come

Autumn holds naked branches high in surrender
grizzly bear tramples to cave,
tucks into bed

Winter

Winter - old man scarred cruel indifferent
The bogeyman
Out there waiting – malicious marauding
Unprepared for fury – sure death
Cross him like the Donner Party
Eat your young
Even the sun hides
Barely peering over mountain ridge

Find shelter like the grizzly
Tucked in his den
Sleeps safely unaware
Solstice comes none too soon
Sun smiles sheepishly
Days get longer
Old man sourly retreats
Those naively ambitious
Not aware
find some tricks still waiting

Last blizzard bellows
Throwing evil trap
Old man scarred cruel indifferent

Spring
is
Pregnant with promise
Days growing longer
Fresh green grass
Baseball's crack of the bat
Every team in first place
Romeo wooing Juliet on the balcony
Adam and Eve in the garden before the snake
Mother Nature nursing babies
African animal's unrestrained
Kids playing in the school yard
Birds, bees, butterflies
bouncing among flowers
touched by the rainbow

Spring
is
Environment nurtured
People without prejudice
Respect required
Laughter infectious
World without war
Disease defeated
Passion pervasive
Love unrestrained – unregretted
Dreams come true

Spring is hope

I wrote the book Finding Shelter from the Cold, about how wolves started to evolve to become dogs during the Last Ice Age.
This fictional account was based on scientific evidence from an ABC News special.

People have said the book reminds them of Jack London. I can have no higher praise.
The Northern California writer is a favorite of mine.
Finding Shelter has been my most popular book.

This next poem and the ones that follow are another way I show my love of nature, wolves and dogs.

Of Men and Gray Wolves

Proud packs of wolves, fathers of our best friend
California's wild side like trees and granite mountains
balanced with nature, prey and predator

Unaware, our fore-fathers built railroads
brought cattle and sheep replacing the buffalo
nature needed to be conquered

There were profits to be made, cut down the trees
another town, or road to be laid, wolves endanger
civilization
cash paid for pelts, hunted harried, until the hills
silent

Those who cared like Mr. Muir, powerless, ignored
in Jack London's native home not a single wolf was left
to roam
nature out of balance, a century without the call of
the wild

Man repented planted a wolf pack in holy sanctuary
Yellowstone
in just a few generations left alone numbers grew for
migrations
last summer a lone gray wild wolf wandered into
California

Will he bring a mate, leave puppies in his den,
a cause for celebration
listen, can you hear howling at the moon,
across granite cliffs, by lagoons

Time is on our wild side, hiking over a mountain
divide,my California child
will hear that native howl, the gray wolf's
call of the wild

A Dog's Life

Four friend's dogs died this week
They're devastated, in mourning
as much as we love our dogs
their lives are too short

Coco an ancient 94 in dog years
bad hips, deaf
can barely walk
needs a guide person

Before Coco
Ripple the wonder dog and
Autumn, Sam's playmate
found doggie heaven
Darn it!

Dog-lives are too short
In dog years I'd be Methuselah

Will I get another?
Sure,
life--short or long is more fun
with a dog

Best Friends

Ripple was wonder-dog
went with me everywhere
when just out of the Navy.

Hiked from Mexico to Canada
and many more times,
curled together in my sleeping bag.

Hitch-hiked to New York and back
quite a sight on Broadway,
he with backpack, me with mine.

"Begador" hippy from East Oakland,
wore a tux his whole life
all black with white boots and shirt
but skipped the bow-tie.
Once ate a whole pan of pot brownies
stayed stoned for a month.
My buddy through college
and teaching days in Turlock.

Colleen and I married
found perfect blond pup
at the Modesto Pound,
a mix of Golden Retriever and Chow.

Named our girl Autumn.
slept with young Sam,
loving family pet
loyal, protective but friendly.

Son sprang up
as Autumn aged
she slowed down.

A stray showed at my school
looked like a young Autumn
but hair black like dark chocolate
named her Coco.

Grumpy elder Autumn
put pup in her place
Coco, Sam's high school companion
matured moved with us to Napa Valley.

Walked with me daily
'til her time sadly ran out.

We rescued Rue
new pooch is settling in
giving us her heart
and a new best friend.

Coco's Final Walk

Coco took a final walk down to the river
passed vines pregnant with purple fruit
eyes mist like morning fog
sadness grabs at my heart

Empty bowl sits on kitchen floor
nevermore to be filled

Goodbye sweet girl
you were loved

The house feels lonely

Who will bark at the mailman

Dog-Gone-IT

Colleen and I splashed over the pass to Santa Rosa on the winding curves of Calistoga Road as the storm's cumulonimbus clouds dumped rivers of water on our car. Like Don Quixote and Esmeralda, we were on a mission and were not about to let another deluge from another rainstorm in this unending wet winter keep us from our quest. A dog named Freckles needed a home and we had been looking for a new canine for weeks and believed the Walking-Tree-Coon Hound was the perfect answer to our search.

GPS determined that we had arrived at the drenched destination of Freckles' temporary host; but the hound rescue lady had not arrived yet. We decided to disembark from our craft and advance to the front door before it floated away.

When we rang the doorbell and the host women opened the door to greet us, Freckles bolted out into the down-pour like a Kentucky Derby filly mudder splashing out of the starting gate. She ran into the flooded street and just missed being flattened by a screech-skidding car. Undeterred and unrestrained the dog splashed past a cattle guard to a soggy field; finally to be caught by the host and my wife with our leash.

Did we take it as a sign of complications to come? Noooo, dog-gone-it! We were on a mission and believed this was just a minor hiccup. While we were chasing the female dog, the rescue lady arrived and told us that Freckles was one of the sweetest dogs she had ever dealt with but should not be let off a leash for a long while. We looked into the baby brown eyes of the three year old hound and saw nothing but sweetness. We were charmed and wanted her. We filled out the adoption form, leashed her in the back of the SUV, weighed anchor and set off to the pet store to buy toys, bones, a bed and dog food.

Back home in Saint Helena that first night, Freckles was an angel, cuddling as we watched TV; later curling into her new bed to fall asleep. The next morning soggy sunshine somehow prevailed and I took our new dog for a mile walk on my usual trail to the Napa River and back. Freckles happily greeted the neighborhood dogs on the walk, securely on leash of course. I got the house ready for me to go to class, moving chocolate candy kisses up in a covered bowl out of her reach on the back of a high counter. Next I fenced her in the kitchen. She could still use the doggy door to go out to the yard. This arrangement had worked well for our previous dog, Coco, who at the ripe old age of sixteen left us for doggy heaven. It also worked for others we dog-sat in our home, but Freckles proved to be a bigger challenge.

I returned to broken glass and half eaten kisses on the kitchen floor. The hound had knocked down the gates and jumped up five feet on the counter. I had under-estimated her potential to get into trouble. Freckles hung her head as if she knew she did something wrong.

"Oh, Freckles, I see you have been a bad girl," I said.

She retreated to the back yard and tried to dig holes under the fence to escape her expected beating. It of course, would never come. That was my first hint that she had been mistreated.

I cleaned up the mess, tried to fill the holes faster then she could dig and get her inside; not an easy task for someone with a bad back and Parkinson's disease.

Just as I was about to call the vet because I knew chocolate was not good for dogs, the phone rang.

"How are things going?" the dog rescue lady asked.

I told her.

She said curtly, "Get her to the vet."

I did.

The vet examined her and told me she looked fine. He gave me his emergency number, and told me to watch her closely. I called the rescue lady back to tell her about the vet visit.

When Colleen came home from work, I filled her in on the day's events. Shortly thereafter, we found out why Freckles was not affected by the chocolate; she puked it up in my closet. Colleen was nice enough to clean it all up. Meanwhile, Freckles took over the couch and refused to get up. She stayed there. I was done, dog tired.

I would try training the hound another day.

Day two, clouds returned. I was going to take Freckles on our walk but I needed to take a chair out of the back of my car to make room for her. The dog coated my back seat with mud the day earlier.

With the pooch lying comfortably on the couch I thought it safe to open the garage to take the chair in.

Want to guess what happened next?

That's right, Freckles was out the doggy door, through the garage and off running. Of course the sky started to pour. I looked for the dog on foot and with the car for hours. I went home hoping she had returned.

She hadn't.

I called Colleen to tell her what happened. Just as I hung up the phone, it rang. You want to guess who was calling?

That's right, it was the rescue lady.

"How's it going today?" She asked.

I told her.

She said, "Why didn't you call me?"

"Because, I was out looking for her."

"I'm coming to get her when she is found," she said indignantly. I'm taking her back.

"Really?" I started to get angry. Despite all the troubles I never thought to give up on the dog. I hung up the phone before I said something I would regret.

The more I thought about it, I realized from her point of view, she was right. Freckles was not the dog for us.

The dog was found at a winery and had not gone far. Her tag still had the rescue number on it. The woman came over the pass in the driving rain to pick Freckles up.

Dog-Gone-IT!

Rue to You Too

We had been looking
for a new dog awhile,
covered many a mile.

She was a new arrival,
waiting to be found
close by at the Napa Pound.

Almost missed her--wasn't around,
she was out walking
luckily we were delayed talking.

Knew right away she was the one,
adopted her on the spot
sorry we are not.

Wears a brown coat
sweet as honey
not much bigger than a bunny.

She's a dog
also a scaredy-cat
but not too frightened to chase a rat

Want to know her name
Just ask she will tell you
in a howl, "Ruuuuuuuuuuue!"

Travel
Don't get around as much as before
never believed I'd take another cruise anymore
but things change—that's for sure.

Majestic Alaska Summer 2015

White crowned mountains multitudes
line up along the rugged coast
like Russian soldiers, uncountable
trees their evergreen uniforms

Hubbard glacier's grandeur
ancient god of ice age
titanic white-blue cold crackles, thunders
sending frozen flows into a thick slurry sea

Eagles soar drafting white-capped ocean winds
looking for life's blood salmon runs
competing with bears, birds, and sea lions
life abounds, otters play, dolphins surf

Solstice artic sunset shines at midnight
rainbow splashes of color
stirring the senses, shimmering
golden like Yukon rush of the last century

I will dream of breaching humpbacks
jumping orcas, splashing blow holes

of Moby Dick,

the howl of white wolves
in Alaska's wild

Big Island Magic

Summer 2017

Hawaiian sun fell into the Pacific Ocean this evening sending colors of rainbows these Islands are famous for, glowing on the western horizon.

Goddess Pele magically steals the sun's heat and light pulling it underground to be released from her volcano as steam, rainbows and flowing molten lava to move back to the sea, and rise the next morning—as that glowing bright ball, completing the miracle daily cycle in this tropical paradise.

*We took this trip to Thailand long before my
Parkinson's but I just got around to writing the poem.*

Thailand The Land of Smiles

Summer 2003

*Thailand exotic, sensual tropical paradise
with food spicy, hot and delicious,
called the land of smiles
populated with happy well fed Buddhists*

*Smells of curry, peanut and pepper
entice traveler's olfactory senses from
elephant and tiger filled forested jungles
to coral seas of warm water beaches*

*Provide peaceful playgrounds of
the proud people of ancient Siam,
loyal and reverent to their King,
never conquered as a Western colony*

*Maybe Thailand was so dear to me
because it was so nice to see
a Southeast Asian country so free*

*Unlike forty years before
when I found myself in the Vietnam War.*

Not Just Going Bananas

Fall 2010

Costa Rica an amazing place
formerly impoverished land
that has changed its very face
to do something amazingly grand

This former banana republic
turned lands into National Parks
making private lands public
an idea that could be a world-wide spark

You can now go ride
over isthmus full of natural wonders
Caribbean Sea on one side
Pacific Ocean on the other

This Central American land
has changed its whole economy
preserved coastal beach sands
and created a new dichotomy

Oldest Democracy on this continent
outlawed the military and shown the way
people can set a special precedent
to live with the biosphere and make a new day

They have proven there is money to be made
where monkeys, birds and reptiles abound
in a place cloud and rain forests provide shade
and we can listen to the call of wild sounds

First Time in Harlem

2005

"123rd Street and Manhattan Avenue please,"
I said to the man as I got in the cab.
He wore a turban and had that Pakistani-Indian accent.
He repeated "123rd and Manhattan?" and looked at me funny,
like I really didn't want to go there.
To dispel his doubt, I said
"Yeah, don't take the Van Wyck,
take the Cross Island to the LIE.
It's faster."
He nodded his head, like OK,
so he really does want to go to Harlem.
Drove too fast, like all New York cabbies.
Weaving in and out of traffic.
Through the Midtown Tunnel,
turned north. bouncing over a curb.
We crossed 123rd Street, I scouted the numbers.
"Here it is, number 152, the brownstone."
He deposited my bags on the curb as I tipped him.
Drove away fast, like he didn't want to be there.

Black face on the street checked out the white guy.
I waved with a smile.
He turned away, thinking tourist. Nobody smiles at
strangers in New York.

Got the key from under the pot and let myself in.
"Nice," I said.
Oak stairway and bannisters reaching five stories
high.
Karen, his Irish-American wife from Hell's Kitchen,
was still at work at the Mayor's Office.
Brother Fred finally home.

"How about Italian," he asked.
"New York Italian, sounds good to me." Mouth
watered.
We walked down his block,
black neighbors waving, saying
"Hey Fred, how ya doing?"
"Good, this is my brutha from California."
I finally got the wave and smile from the locals.
We crossed Columbia University to Broadway
and headed downtown.
Fred, baby daughter Grace in arms,
into the crosswalk.
Car cheated past the white line.
Fred pounded on the hood.

"Hey asshole, can't you see I'm walkin'
here with my daughta?"
Yeah, it's good to be back in New York.

I've been to Paris three times and love it, one of my favorite cities. I wrote this after the first terrorist attack on that wondrous place.

A Love Letter to Lady Paris

She came from the tennis courts
red clay clicked off white shoes
downy mist showing through her shirt
ducks into the shower drain bleeds red

I love the notion of her
her words sound somehow sexy
like saxophone playing jazzy Gershwin
on the bank of the Seine

The woman dresses just right
making the most of the gods gifts
skirt slit with one side showing
just enough stockinged leg

She smells delicious
lilacs, roses and a taste of cayenne pepper
champagne open on the table
I joke, she laughs till she cries

Her eyes deep green-blue pools
like sunny waters of Mediterranean Sea
where she walks proudly topless
swims and wades ashore like Venus

The lady skis expertly in her Alps
can cook a five course dinner
in the shadows of the Eiffel Tower
she peers into my soul

"Je tiem," she says sexually
we dance on the balcony
never make it to dinner
shots ring out in the streets

Getting Philosophical and Political

I wrote this first poem just before getting DBS for Parkinson's

Deep Space Exploration

Prose can be fiction
poetry is truth
heart and soul

Next week MRI
then Deep Brain Stimulation

Probing deep
tangled neurons
like a crazy
sci-fi story

What me worry
it's not like brain surgery
or rocket science
Oh yeah, it is

What will the explorers find
in that neuron universe
prose or poetry
or just silence?

Freedom vs Fate

Free will versus fate
it's been such a long debate
I was lucky to live in the land of the free
no Hitler or Stalin around to control me
yet there was a draft you didn't chose
if your number came up you lose
you knew before you went
such useless blood being spent
did the people of North Vietnam
choose to be under Nixon's bombs
would we make the same choice again
I don't believe so my friends

Now 40 years later
fate caused another story to arise
Parkinson's would cause my physical demise
I believed I would play tennis until my heart give out
ski and hike mountains majesty's glory
unfortunately that's not the story
instead I take time
write free verse or rhyme
fate you see is not always kind
I still want to be
meeting every day with glee
with friends, writing prose and poetry
that's my way to be free

They Think--Therefore They Are-- I Think

Remember the Jetson's TV show
with flying cars and robots everywhere?
That future's much closer than you know
in some ways we are almost there.

It's true our autos don't fly around
be it Ford, Honda, BMW, or Chevy
gravity keeps them all stuck on the ground.

Yet if you're going to mountains or river levy,
a driver soon won't be needed
artificial intelligence will drive your car.
It seems that we have succeeded
creating robots that can decide near or far.

I don't know how comfortable I feel
about machines that believe they can think.
What if they tried to deal
with politics and take us to the brink,
of nuclear destruction and total annihilation?

Did the robot creators remember the sci-fi Asimov
rule
and put "do no harm to humans" in the equation?
Maybe we need to program them to; don't be cruel.

Two Neverlands

Part 1

One side effect of Parkinson's disease
is how it attacks my dream machine.
Dreams become very real
as the brain deals with lack of dopamine.
Lashing out at night time enemies,
I have knocked over lamps and screamed
from nightmares that seem very real
to protect my dear wife
I've moved away from nighttime warmth
to a separate bed in another room
to deal with the gloom of night
If I don't awake after bad dreams
I can't remember why I scream
But if I do wake in the middle of the night
I remember vividly what causes my fear
I've dreamed of hiking in snow waist deep
fighting foes big and small,
hand to hand, with guns or swords
or falling, falling never to land
In Mr. Sandman's Neverland

Part II

Lately, I have a recurring dream
with a 1984 type theme.
A crazed man is elected king,
takes away minority rights,
builds wall like medieval castles,
and turns down Lady Liberty's light.
His goose stepping voters still take his side
Say, "It don't matter if you're Christian and white."
The king and his cohorts could care less
About Mother Nature's plight;
he will rake in lots of money
from big oil and smokestack's greed.
King dictator ignores hurricanes, tornadoes
with power never seen before
will he notice when both coasts
and Gulf States are under water?
People march against this dilemma.
King tweets to them,
"Bring it on, I'm ready to fight."
Please let me wake from this nightmare
but dawn is nowhere on the horizon.

Gray

Morning sky covered in Gray
matching mood on this day
suddenly light blinked bright
soon the gray went away

Sun rose be gone the night
Still wondered if I'd be all right
Didn't want to feel so alone
Every day I had to fight

Battled demons on my own
Far away I had to roam
I looked to somehow see
far from my home

and pay the fee
find a way to be free
knew that was the key
to be what was left of me

After the Fall

Lunacy
sunset's regret
drowns in ocean
moonglow shadows
black and white
so cold

Paint pools
colors on the ground
leaving
limbs so bare
tears like winter rain

So cold
moonglow shadows
black and white
shiver
after the fall
lunacy

Prejudice and Pride

Are you are prejudiced?
I am.
Surprised?
You are also.
We all are.
Think about you own prejudice.
Everyone has feelings of discomfort.
Recognize where it come from--FEAR!
Have pride,
be brave,
rise above it.
Forgive yourself.
All you need is love

What I can't forget:

Pat Nixon's cloth coat; JFK's Camelot; ML King at the mountain top; LBJ all the way; Last helicopter out of Saigon; One small step; Watergate hotel; The Beatles on Ed Sullivan; Bobby winning the California Primary; The night the lights went out in NY; Not a Lincoln but a Ford; Hostages in Iran; Trickle down; Desert Storm; Bill Clinton's cigar; Two Towers; Invading Iraq; A first black president; Getting Trumped

I wrote a Young Adult book called Roger Raintree's Seventh Grade Blues; it took place in St. Louis. That very summer the Ferguson riot took place. I added a chapter called Summertime Blues and penned this poem.

Prelude to Summertime Blues

Jazz, blues, rock 'n roll
rhythms toll
out where St. Louis streets lie
music sweet mix homogenize
counter cultures of the hot city
fed by waters mighty Mississippi
along banks of great river
night swelters, stew pot simmers
ready to boil over burning everyone
after midnight a different song sung
drumbeats like gunshots, RAP screams
bursting at the seams
where gangsters roll
police do not control
in Ferguson, guns bark
black man-boy lies in the dark
white cop finds weapons-not
as the sun rises blood red hot

sky hazy thick covered in sweat
a mom and dad sit at home and fret
crickets sing background soulful song
in suburban town everything goes wrong
care not skin black or white
a mosquito finds red blood to bite.

Hope

January 12, 2015

In Oakland and Ferguson protests turn to riots and
confusion
People of color and police fight without a solution
Was this Dr. King's dream as he put pen to page
Walls built around factions of people like towns during
the Dark Ages
In the city of light and love there is no resolution
No one listening, no common ground, just hate and
disunion
The forces of fear, and hate must disengage
Not react with abandoned rage
We need a new messiah with vision so vast
When people read and hear the words
they will put down their guns and swords
There will be peace on earth at last
I can cope with hope
My pen has hope

This poem won third prize out of 1400 entries in the Voices of Lincoln Poetry Contest in 2017.

Of Dreams

Dr. Martin Luther King Jr.'s Dream
included the notion
his children could live in a nation
not be judged by the color of their skin,
but the content of their character.
Are the two Obama elections what he saw from the
mountain top?
After the election
I had my own dream.
Autumn, my golden lab said to Coco, my black lab,
"Can you believe that people care so much about the
color of ones coat?"
"No, that's so dumb. Dogs would never do that.
When I smell another dogs butt
we all look about the same."

Whether Report

I can't tell if I'm watching the Weather Channel or
CNN
It's colder with a chance of Heat-in Paris expect rain
of terror-worldwide climate change predicted-
California summer saw drought driven fires-El Nino
rain this winter-Record rainfall in Texas-Trump up 10
degrees-Hillary down 5 percentage points-a reign of
bullets hit. So Cal-snow blizzards assault the Midwest-
largest hurricane in Mexico-cop kills unarmed black
man-police shoot American born terrorist and wife-
baby survives-mudslides-tornado tears up Mississippi
town-windy with a chance of fog-balmy bombs in
Beirut-Cold War returns to Moscow-smog thick in
Beijing-earthquakes with warming trend in Chile.

I push the button but it won't turn off

Amoral Compass

The boy grew up big and strong
watching the news on CBS
did cause him much distress
he realized Vietnam War was wrong

but his number was called
and from his plane
bombs fell like rain
people were killed or mauled

Sorry about killing sons and daughters
as the deads names were read
I'm not guilty, he said
you see, I was just following orders

Election Day Blues

I'm thinking there has to be a better way.
Two years of spending tons of money
what we get is not very funny.

Just look at the precident,
Buchanan, Hoover, George Bush #2,
not an impressive list; to name a few.

Then there was Nixon the famous crook,
not so smart or very nice,
so what the heck, we elected him twice.

Jefferson, that champion of freedom owned slaves.
Jackson on the twenty dollar bill
killed Indians in waves.

When it cost millions for a job that pays thousands,
is it any wonder my son refuses to choose?
"Any way you look at it," he says, "we lose."
And hope Trump card doesn't have us singing the
blues

All the News That Fits

Have you heard the latest news from the president
He wants to set a new precedent.
Send a special group of illegal aliens
Back from whence they came.
Many never played football or baseball,
but some other strange game.
They arrived with no visas or passports
and are uniquely different.
From crafts traveling from places very distant,
the president saw them on tv last night,
causing all kinds of problems and plight.
They are killing Americans with weapons of mass destruction,
Destroying buildings with different types of construction.
Yes, they are over here invading American dreams,
Making us wake up and scream.
Not Muslims, but a much more deadly force.
He's talking about Martians and spacemen of course,
Plotting their evil ways,
with proton torpedoes and death rays.

He says, "Never mind, there is one super from Krypton and he is kind."
"Oh no!" he cries,
"The guy is a secret reporter full of lies.

Probably writing fake news right now,
which of course, I can't allow.
He's got to go; can't be trusted,
Get Homeland Security, he must be busted."

This story must be true, one we can't overlook.

Last night I read it on my Facebook.

Strange Daze

The same year Bob Dylan wins Nobel Prize,

Donald Trump is elected President of the United Stated of America.

Certainly gods of Karma are angry and messing with us.

Change is blowing in the wind with hurricane force.

The Donald wants to gut the EPA, the Department of Education,

and build a wall between California and Mexico.

Instead he needs to build a sea wall for the rising ocean due to climate

change that his anti-environment agenda will advance.

Good luck all you American women, your bodies no longer your own.

I can't keep track of the changes without a score card.

What next?

Maybe, California secedes from the Union with the rest of the left coast,

New England, New Jersey and New York join Canada.

Maybe, the rest becomes the Confederate States of America.

Just maybe, the Confederates outlaw Protest Rock and make Country Music the official music of the new CSA ruled by Dictator Trump.

Canada builds a wall to keep the Confederates out.

The Confederates and Russia declare war on Canada. Mexico, Cuba and the rest of NATO aligns with Canada.

American football and NASCAR are outlawed in Canada

Soccer is outlawed in the new Confederacy.

You don't think so?

I tell you strange stuff is happening.

Custer Died For Our Sins

Western train throws a loud whistle
but bison won't be moved
car screeches to a whiplash halt

Buffalo hunters emerge
bringing down great beasts
too many to count
a hole appears
showing the endless tracks beyond

Locomotive belches black cloud
starts slowly, picking up speed
White way west
Lakota Nation weeps

One hundred fifty years later
it is not tracks that scar Dakota land
but a pipeline
oil way south

Lakota Nation weeps

Happy Holidays Poems

Thanksgiving
2017

Redwood forest covered hills
movies and books that thrill
autumn's colors on grape leaves
puppy dogs that retrieve
a bird with sweet song
when its mate sings along
golden glow sunrise and set
rivers flowing by, deep, quick, wet
watching the ocean's powerful surf
sunny day, music plays, lying on turf
the smell of dinner as it cooks
family, friends by hook or by crook
for all this I am so very thankful
let's toast and eat another mouthful

Candlelight

2015

T'was the last Hanukkah night
candles gave off a sweet light
the cabin all aglow
for our family at Lake Tahoe

We played in the High Sierra snow
where the cold winds blow
skied down steep runs
almost having too much fun

Son Sam counted his gelt
each day I had dealt
I asked Colleen if she wanted white or red
with the Chinese take-out we were fed

It had been a wonderful stay
over the long holiday
no matter how far we roamed
if we were with each other
we were home

Missing Dirty Snow

2016

Christmas in New York,
people rushing here and there,
hailing a cab, catching the subway,
neon lights of Broadway,
with all the plays,
Macys' window displays,
Central Park's Children's Zoo,
family members who have passed away from you,
trains at Grand Central or Penn Station,
taking people to suburbs or across the nation,
Rockefeller plaza with the tree ablaze
and skates on ice,
buying pizza by the slice,
pastrami on rye sandwiches and a potato knish,
meatball heroes filling up a whole dish,
smelling Chestnuts roasting,
served with hot cider for toasting.
Sometimes I miss the Big Apple
right down to the core.

Happy Spring Equinox

Have you ever wondered where

the Easter bunny got the magic eggs?

I heard he followed Alice's white rabbit

down that psychedelic hole

grabbed some tea with the Mad Hatter

and they all sang rock and roll.

One egg made you larger,

one made you small,

one colored magic egg would

save you from the Queen of Hearts

if in the hole you ever fall.

Family Musings

Time and Teapots

Some people are frozen in time
like John F. Kennedy or Marilyn Monroe
alive back in the 60's
never to get old

When I left home at eighteen
Cousin Abby was a little girl
doing the teapot dance
in the living room of our youth

Yet the spell can be broken
time can race ahead
just because you didn't notice
the clock keeps ticking

Dr. Abby came to visit last week
with her second husband
and stories of her three adult kids
time played its game

Crows walked on our faces
what doesn't die young, grows old
little teapot illusion
lies shattered on the living room floor

Ashes

The box containing his ashes
arrived in the mail
like something ordered from amazon
I got half; he wanted them scattered
in two of his favorite places,
Napa Valley and Hawaii

I carried fine grain powder and
poured it on the west bank of
the Napa river, where a day before
I watched a big coyote splash across

A week earlier that dust was the body
of step-brother Fred, who's taunting quick wit
tortured me through high school,
yet I grew to love and even admire him

The west wind blew his ashes into the river
flowing down to San Francisco Bay and beyond
I think he would have liked that last journey
out the Golden Gate to the Pacific Ocean
to surf with seals and great white sharks

Southwestern Woman

The Rio Grande flows through
canyon walls - red rusty New Mexican sandstone
sedimentary rock built by grains of sand
like her life exposed to the elements

Tears flow like raindrops
streams that become the river
cross a crooked path
to and away from love

Three tributaries merge
at Albuquerque
flow into dangerous rapids
desperately
she hangs on

Holiday Cheer—2016

All's well in Wine County
Autumn rains have turned the hills bright green
This morning on my walk to the river
the air is fresh and clean.

As for my health.
for the most part I am all right,
Parkinson's shakes and stiffenings
don't leave me too uptight.

I was able to endure a plane ride
to So-Cal,
spend some time with the in-laws,
just twelve of them
not the full tide;
a good time was had.

But of Christmas tunes
I've had my fill.
If I hear any more
a reindeer I will kill

Hope to see you all soon
but some are not so near.
So wishing you
a happy and healthy New Year

My love for sports continues...

The Sporting Life

I didn't play ball
until age 9, moved to Green Acres
then I never stopped,
loved all the games

For friends and me at Forest Road School
there were only three seasons:
baseball, football and basketball,
in order of importance.

Baseball started just after the snow melt
slapball, stickball, softball at the schoolyard
Mel Allen and Red Barber
familiar voices from Florida

Majors moved north with summer sweat
TV's tuned to channel 9 and 11
soon Little Leagues
replaced improvised fun

No Peter Pans, we grew up
separating boys from men
in high school football
passed baseball in passion

Cheerleader's curves replaced
the ones thrown with two fingers
basketball followed
little guys left behind

Played JV pigskin
helmet and pads
tackle tore my meniscus
moving me from fields of youth

To wrestle in obscurity
or cruise to Nathan's
new driver's license
and a draft card

After Vietnam and the Navy
played soccer, tennis in college
skied the Sierra
coached a new generation

Never stopped playing
couldn't quit
until Parkinson's fell on the fumble
and the balls quit bouncing

Who That Foe From?

2014

Fee fi foe fum, I smell the blood of a Royal?

What the he-ll is a roya-ll

From Webster: family of king or queen especially

English

So, fee fi foe from-Queens, not Dodgers from Brookyln?

Both blue, but Royal Blue?

Hard to get my knickers in a twist for Royal Blue

But it is the serious World Series, so

Fee fi foe fum, I smell the blue blood of an Englishman

Eat 'em up Giants

A Stacked Deck

The Royal war raged
for seven nights and days
fought by great
and powerful knights.

One knight stood
above the rest
sword swinging in left hand
defeated royal knights
from all the lands.

Late in the game
the King finally came
he knew every trick
sword very quick.

The ace trumped the King
with a mighty giant swing
royal blood did run blue
the people now knew.

The King is dead,
long live the King
Madison the 1st will reign over the land
ancestor of ancient King
Christy Mathewson*
O'r the castle by the bay
A pennant raised to fly another day.

*Hall of Fame Giant's Pitcher

Its 2015 and the Warriors are NBA Champs and set A Golden Record

Let us all lift a toast
to the team with the most
you would think it would be hard to relate
to the team, Golden State

But in tee's that say: The City
they look oh so pretty
raining down threes and
playing D like swarms of bees

with a game on the line
spicy Curry says, it's mine
the quickest shot in the west
shows why he is now the best

The shot goes in
Warriors have another win
three beats two every time
Splash Brother's shooting so sublime

The Bull's with MJ so great
but they were resigned to fate
to the new best team
playing hoops like a dream

YOGI

He was the Yogi of baseball
a mystical character
beyond the Hall of Fame
ten World Series rings, three MVP's
catching the perfect, perfect game

He played just before my time
already a legend
World War II hero
baseball god

There was just one Yogi
a genuine master guru
never made sense
until the double take

Words, like Don Larson's curve ball
that legendary day
looking out of the strike zone
until it fell in Yogi's mitt

"It ain't over till it's over;
Can't hit and think at the same time;
A nickels not worth a dime anymore;
Practice is the best practice;
Nobody goes there anymore,
It's too crowded;
I never said half the stuff I said."

It ain't over Yogi, people will quote you like
Shakespeare

He may have been a lifelong Yankee, but he was a
Giant

The Music Muse

A Rhapsody for George Gershwin in Blue

First saw **An American in Paris** on TV
when Gene Kelly and lovely Lesley Caron
danced through Paris, fell in love with the movie
music stayed with me, brought record home.

When I heard **Rhapsody in Blue**,
the music grabbed my very soul,
written by the same man who
showed those Paris dancers their role.

Never heard anything like it before
classical and jazz fusion
was something I could adore
created a great mental illusion.

Next I heard **Porgy and Bess**
as Martin Luther King Jr and the rest
were deep in the Alabama mess
fighting against that Southern hornets' nest.

George died age 39, in 39
but bugle boys carried his muse;
liberated Paris, crossed the Rhine.
Hitler outlawed jazz, was bound to lose.

George sat with Rosa on the bus;
at Woodstock--played with Hendrix; the blues,
he marched against the Vietnam War with us;
his music in my head, I've walked miles in his shoes.

This Concerto Never Ends

Ladies dressed in grand gowns
men in bright blue uniforms
dance the minuet to Fur Elise
in Fredrick the Great's
Berlin Palace ballroom
outside birds and bees
swarming spring flowers
in solitude and sunshine
cannons boom breaking
the sweet serenity
dancers scatter as shells shatter
"To Arms," the general commands
Napoleon sits atop his steed
looking with spyglass
as his troops storm in
the piano player keeps
playing somehow
now the army is Russian
the dress camouflage
from Second World War
overrunning bombed out Berlin
Beethoven's piano concerto
like another generation of soldiers
sadly plays on

Dancing Fool

I love to dance the night away
Like Gene Kelly or Fred Astaire
Be it swing, disco or rock and roll
Musical rhythms get my feet tapping

Glen Miller, Louis Armstrong, Beatles, Rolling Stones
Drums beat, horns blast, guitar wails
I loved to dance the night away
Musical rhythms got my feet tapping

Over, under, kick left then right
She slides through my legs
This girl's so tight, does everything right
Musical rhythms got my feet tapping

I love to dance the night away

Classic—Classical Rock

If Beethoven were alive today
would he still write
in classical mode?
I think not.
What would he write?
Rock, Blues, Jazz, Punk, Rap?
Or would the greatest musician ever
find something totally unique?
Maybe an electric fifth symphony
he on piano—rock it with Clapton on guitar.
Whatever—please buy me a ticket.

My home extends to the Sierra, where I had so many good times hiking and skiing and where Colleen and I got married.
This is a story about a couple who found the mountains quite challenging.

Over the Granite Rocks

Winter in the Sierra, fine white drifts of snow piled

high, over the basilisk of granite rocks,

Blowing in the wind, like the answers in that Bob

Dylan sixties song;

while the two young lovers, Maria and John,

off skiing that morning at Alpine Meadows,

way above turquoise-blue Lake Tahoe;

crossed over the ridge to Squaw Valley's steep and

deep.

That afternoon; laughing and flying down the

sunshine bright powder,

all the while always drinking, drinking, wine,

bota bag tequila—so drunk, stumble fall into the

Ford—drive and in one deep breath, car skidding on

frozen, black ice to take wing, flying like a bird.

No—more like that jet with engines destroyed by birds

which crash-landed in the Hudson River,

But unlike that happy ending, in this Romeo and

Juliet sad story, the perfectly frozen bodies would not

be found until spring when ripples of melted snow

flowed over the granite rocks.

Drugs and other musings.

Mary-Jane

I smoked Marijuana.
Not really a revelation is it?
As Bob Dylan said, "Everybody must get stoned."
Couldn't go anywhere in the 70's
without someone passing you a joint.
Pot went great with music
 gave you the munchies.
Was a whole lot of fun
But made me feel stupid,
so like Hoyt Axton's sentiment,
I sang along
No I don't smoke it no more...
tired of waking up on the floor

Talking about stupid; was its prohibition
tried that with booze,
didn't work so well.
Seen a lot of mean drunks,
not many mean stoners,
unless they were drunk

Nostalgic Romance

Without Direction

She looked like absolute perfection
sunning topless on the campus lawn, so free
blue eyes reflecting cloudless California sky
a waterfall of blond hair streaming down her back,
captivating me

Carefully I came from east, casting no shadow
smiling she beckoned I sit
the lady studied art
history my habit

We loved like Romeo and Juliet
without objection from family masses
unabashed passion red hot
dancing 'till dawn, or classes

Out of nowhere came the disagreement
she said north with some conviction
I argued for south stating my objection
so we went different directions
somehow forgetting
summer sun's beauty sets west

What is the Perfect Kiss?

Is it light and breezy
like the wind on a summer's day?
Or filled with passion,
a growing storm,
full of electric thunder and lightning?
Is it Eskimos in an igloo in Alaska touching noses
bringing warmth while everything freezes outside?
Or in Hawaii where touching lips
can cause the volcano to erupt.
Is it the first kiss with someone of the same-sex,
that sets a gay person free?
Two teenagers making out in the back seat
'till lips are sore and still they kiss more?
Or a French Kiss with a touch
of tongue that says amore?
Is it two movie stars kissing on a the silver screen,
sending people home happy, all warm and fuzzy?
A solder kissing his bride
after being away fighting a war?
Is it a tease, a promise of passion?
Still I wonder
what is the perfect kiss?

Worth More than a Thousand Words

There is a photo in a picture-book
from the year nineteen seventy-one
of Jenny, who truly loved me
She had a smile bright as California summer sun
brown eyes sprinkled with gold specks that sparkled
beauty in full bloom, prettier, a perfect rose,
and kisses tasty as chardonnay
her cute Southern accent
melted my Yankee heart
as we walked hand in hand in Tilden Park
But I could only love her for a little while
she wanted and deserved so much more
my friends all thought I was crazy
to turn my back on her loving arms
they were close to the truth
I had a secret flaw
Which hurt me more,
losing my mother at seven
or my angry stepmom?
No regrets, found my mate
almost twenty years later
yet it's hard not to wonder
about the road not taken.

Romancing Colleen (some more)

Amazing

You are amazing, green eyed woman,
make me happy when I'm blue,
when I think I can't, I can, because of you

Your sweet love's all I ever need
Come back baby don't make me plead

You brighten my every day
when storm clouds threaten
you simply blow them away

Your sweet love's all I ever need
Come back baby, don't make me plead

If you're gone the sun won't shine
the world is dark and gray
baby please-please tell me you're mine

Your sweet love's all I ever need
Come back baby, don't make me plead

Come back my sweet baby,
Don't make me plead
I'm down, down, down
on my hands and knees

Ocean Devotion

I want to make love to you like a tropical ocean
envelope you in warm water's embrace
waves of pleasure move with a passion
fill your body with my devotion
alter the motion and pace
no one made love to you in this fashion
touch you with kiss after kiss
lips with sexy salty taste
tell me you love this
float in orgasmic bliss

When You're Gone,

I miss you like I miss the sun
on this cold rainy day.

My mind drifts back:
to the magic of summer solstice
the ship sailing south
Alaska's inlet passage
mystic mountains reached skyward port and
starboard
eastern mounts reflecting never ending sunset
western sun peered above peaks
refusing surrender of its golden perch
making a pact with night to stay away
light came through sky's prism
casting multi-colors above blue horizon.

This longest day you played with sea otter.
I walked along the coastal forest
leaves green as Irish grass.
We watched eagles take wing.

Dining late
Oysters Rockefeller and lobster
me wearing tails
you glamorously gowned

witnessing a pod of orca breaching
out the portside window
swimming alongside the ship.

Starboard side stateroom
you sat on the balcony
black gown pulled above your knee
showing your pretty legs
watching humpbacks in the distance
last rays backlighting
giving you a golden crown
like a princess.

Midnight sun setting behind mountains
still tossing a distant glow.
"The sun will rise too soon," I said.
"Close the curtains and come to bed,
still some magic to be played this night."
You fall into my arms.

I still feel lucky in love.
Please hurry home!
I miss you like I miss the sun
on this cold rainy day.

These next writings didn't quite fit into the categories of the others.

Just Romeing Around

Jules sees her across the room
felt like a man bewitched
her olive skin, head held high,
black mini-dress, long legs

She of shimmering locks
topped with a tiara and
penetrating royal blue eyes
knifing into his heart

They met at the Rubicon River Tavern
she smiled a killer smile, said her name was Cleo
he knew there was no turning back
from this wondrous woman

Danced, glided together
feet never touched the ground
two moved as one, full of grace

Jules tasted Cleo's luscious lips
melting into each other's arms
sensually, exploding in passion

But morning came, the ides of March
Cleo retreated to Cairo and her
loveless marriage to a brutus,
queen for only one blissful night

Jules left with wingman Mark Anthony
feeling stabbed in the back
dark glasses battled bright sunshine
and hid a single tear

"Which way?" Mark asked.

Jules shrugged, "All roads lead to Rome."

January 17, 2015

God's heavenly counsel: Gandhi, Moses, Mohamed, Jesus and Buddha were hearing the big guy rant again.
"Can't those earthling get anything right?
I said swords into plowshares not make IUD's."

"That's IEDs Lord," Mohamed reminded him

"Who can keep track of all the stuff they make to kill each other?"
Maybe it's time to send another message, or even smite some of them, for gosh sakes, blowing up Paris, really my divine Paris, so beautiful." He shook his head.
The Lord continued, "It's been a while since I actually got involved and talked to that guy Smith in upstate N.Y. I like what his followers built in that desert in Utah but they still got it wrong, When I told him, to have them multiply I was being literal; their SAT math scores needed improvement. I did not mean take more wives and have more babies."
Moses said, "Let's do the 15 commandment thing again that worked the last time—oh yeah...maybe not. So are you going to do the smite thing."

"No." God said, "Let's wait another year, I heard the Cubs might be good this year. It's been 103 years since they won a World Series and I only made your people Moses, wait 40 to get to the Promised Land. I'd like to see them actually win. Then the Olympics in Moscow, I'd love to see the Bolshoi ballet. Beside if we wait a few more years of them ignoring Climate Change they will be mostly under water."

"Many of mine and your American Christians don't believe that." Jesus reminded him.

"Either did Noah, at first!" God declared.

Perils of being a wise-guy

Wise wrinkles on woman's face were earned
her words like a dissertation

Granddaughter all fresh and perky
knew not what she was yet to learn
many mistakes resulted

When I shared my observations
both walked away insulted

It's the Invasion of the Body Snatchers

Seems like no one gets out alive
They are not Zombies
but they are mutants
some so very small, invisible
silent but deadly
there are thousands,
no millions, no billions of 'em
going up our noses
sneaking into our mouths
from our food
attacking our organs
viruses, bacteria, protozoa

and one damn mosquito
buzzing around my room
like she owns the place
biting all night long
robing me of sleep and sanity

The Advantages of having Parkinson's Disease in California

1. Can't smell dog poo when picking it up.

2. Don't need to put a quarter in magic fingers in cheap motels.

3. Handicap Parking sticker

4. Earthquake, what earthquake?

5. Medical marijuana

6. Turbulence, what turbulence?

7. Don't have to worry about getting jitters from another cup of coffee

8. No one mentions that stain on my shirt

9. Great at making James Bond a martini

10. Have a great excuse for making typoss (You may have noticeed)

ABOUT THE AUTHOR

Nathaniel Robert "Bob" Winters, grew up in suburban N.Y.C. Upon completing a tour in the Navy, he fell in love with and settled in Northern California. Bob earned a BA with a major in history, with minors in geography and biology from Sonoma State University; and a Master's in Educational Counseling from CSU Stanislaus.

The retired teacher lives with his wife/muse, Colleen and dog, Rue in the Napa Valley. Son, Sam is attending UCLA.

Despite having Parkinson's disease, he writes almost every day and has published sixteen books in the last ten years. His prose and poetry have won awards and can be found in many anthologies and of course, in his books.

The books of Nathaniel Robert Winters

Something for everyone:

Children and Young Adult:
The Substitute—A children's story of Winter's Holidays

Roger Raintree's 7ᵗʰ Grade Blues—Young adult: A fun modern early teen adventure with relevant lessons to be learned in each chapter.

Finding Shelter from the Cold—Young Adult and adults that have a love for dogs— Ice age fictional story about wolves becoming dogs. Its source was an ABC nature film using DNA evidence. Will remind the reader of Jack London's Call of the Wild

Adult Novels:
The Adventures of the Omaha Kid—Romance, adventure, sports, triumph and tragedy

Penngrove Ponderosa—Story of Sonoma State University students in the early 70's—sex, drugs, rock—with the shadow of Vietnam in the background.

Sci-fi:
>*Past the Future*—Space ships, baby factories, clones, time machines--just for starters. Will Dave save the world?

>*Black Knight of Berkeley*—Evil doers Beware, *The Black Knight* is after you.

Poetry and short stories:
>*The Poet I Didn't Know*
>*Daydream Diversions*
>*Another Revolution*

Memoir and Biography:
>*Rumors about my Father*—Gangsters, depression WWII—Oh my

>*No Place for a Wallflower*—Story of a brave woman during WWII

>*Legend of Heath Angelo*—Started the first Nature Conservancy Preserve in CA.

>*Not Quite Kosher*—Bob's story

The Richard R. Hegner Story—Life of a Vietnam Hero

The Substitute—A Children's Winter Holiday Story

Made in the USA
San Bernardino, CA
28 September 2017